SPECTRUM® READERS

ROAR!
Big Cats

By Lisa Kurkov

Carson-Dellosa Publishing

An imprint of Carson-Dellosa Publishing, LLC
P.O. Box 35665
Greensboro, NC 27425-5665

carsondellosa.com

Printed in the USA. All rights reserved.
ISBN 978-1-4838-0115-5

01-002141120

Big cats roam the wild.
They purr and roar.
They leap and hunt.
Big cats are powerful!

Bobcat

This big cat is
a bobcat.
Bobcats are twice
as big as house cats.
They eat small
animals.

Cougar

This big cat is
a cougar.
Once, cougars roamed
the United States.
Today, they live in
only a few places.

Lynx

This big cat is
a lynx.
Lynxes have very
good eyesight.
They have good
hearing, too.

Ocelot

This big cat is
an ocelot.
Ocelots live in Central
and South America.
They are good swimmers.

Leopard

This big cat is
a leopard.
Leopards hide
in trees.
When they see prey,
they pounce!

Clouded Leopard

This big cat is a
clouded leopard.
Clouded leopards
are good climbers.
They can hang
upside down!

Snow Leopard

This big cat is a
snow leopard.
Snow leopards have
warm, thick fur.
Their furry feet act
like snowshoes.

Black Panther

This big cat is a
black panther.
Black panthers have
spots, but they are
very hard to see!
They hunt at night.

Jaguar

This big cat is
a jaguar.
Jaguars are good
swimmers.
Sometimes, they eat
fish and turtles.

Bengal Tiger

This big cat is a
Bengal tiger.
Tigers need our help.
More live in zoos
and parks than in
the wild!

Siberian Tiger

This big cat is a
Siberian tiger.
At night, tigers hunt.
They can eat 60 pounds
of meat a day!

African Lion

This big cat is a lion.
Lions roar very loudly.
They can be heard
five miles away!

Cheetah

This big cat is
a cheetah.
Cheetahs are the
fastest land animals.
They can run
70 miles per hour!

Cats

Big cats are wild
and beautiful.
The next time you
pet a house cat,
think of its amazing
cousins!

ROAR! Big Cats
Comprehension Questions

1. What do bobcats eat?

2. Where did cougars used to live?

3. Why do you think lynxes are good hunters?

4. Where do ocelots live?

5. What do clouded leopards do well?

6. What keeps snow leopards warm?

7. When do black panthers hunt?

8. What do jaguars sometimes eat?

9. Are there more tigers in the wild or in zoos and parks?

10. How far away can a lion's roar be heard?

11. What is the fastest land animal?